BRAINPOWER

# YOUR BRAIN WHEN YOU'RE ANGRY

BY ABBY COLICH

T0014930

BLUE OWL
BOOKS

# TIPS FOR CAREGIVERS

Social and emotional learning (SEL) helps children manage emotions, learn how to feel empathy, create and achieve goals, and make good decisions. One goal of teaching SEL skills is to help children understand what is going on in their bodies and brains when they experience certain emotions. The more children understand, the more easily they may be able to regulate their emotions and empathize with others.

## BEFORE READING

Talk to the readers about what makes them feel angry and any physical changes they notice in their bodies when they are angry.

**Discuss:** Think about a time when you felt angry. How did your body feel?

## AFTER READING

Talk to the readers about changes that take place in their brains when they feel angry.

**Discuss:** What happens in your brain when you feel angry? What is one way you can help yourself feel better when you are angry?

## SEL GOAL

Children may struggle with processing their emotions, and they may lack accessible tools to help them do so. Explain to children that changes take place in their brains when they feel strong emotions. These changes can affect how their bodies feel. Certain actions can trigger changes in the brain that help them feel better.

# TABLE OF CONTENTS

**CHAPTER 1**
Feeling Angry...................................................4

**CHAPTER 2**
Anger in Your Brain.......................................8

**CHAPTER 3**
Manage Your Anger.....................................14

**GOALS AND TOOLS**
Grow with Goals..........................................22
Try This!.........................................................22
Glossary........................................................23
To Learn More.............................................23
Index..............................................................24

# CHAPTER 1

# FEELING ANGRY

Can you think of a time you felt angry? Anger is an **emotion**. People can feel angry when they think they are treated unfairly, are **frustrated**, or are feeling **unappreciated**.

Your body may get **tense**. You may **clench** your fists or jaw. Your face may get red.

Your heart may beat faster.
You might breathe quicker.
You may have more **energy**.

Your vision becomes sharper.
Your attention **focuses**. Why?
These changes prepare your
body for a fight, flight, or
freeze response.

## FIGHT, FLIGHT, OR FREEZE

How does fight, flight, or freeze work?
If you are arguing with someone,
for example, your brain kicks into
action. It tells you to either keep
arguing (fight), run away (flight),
or do nothing (freeze).

# CHAPTER 2

# ANGER IN YOUR BRAIN

Your brain is like a control center for your emotions. When something makes you angry, it **triggers** a part of your brain called the amygdala.

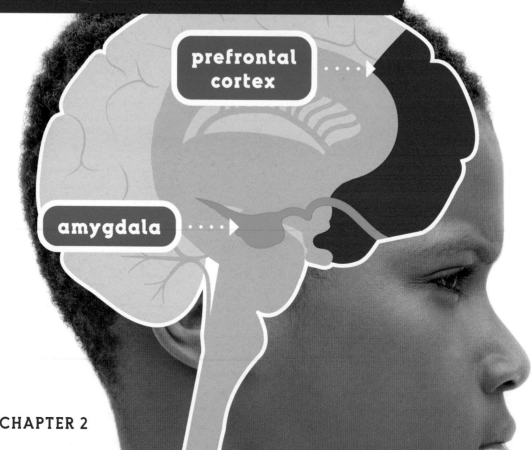

prefrontal cortex

amygdala

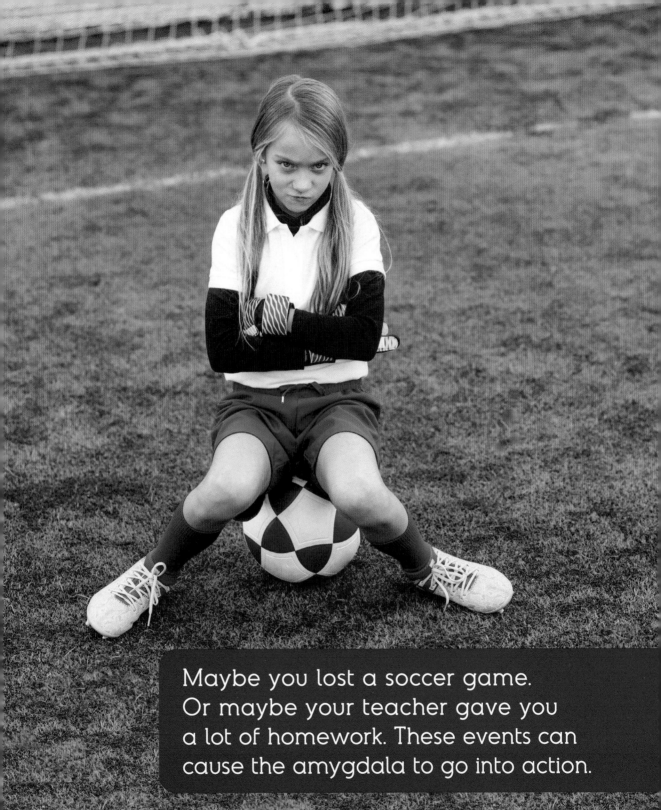

Maybe you lost a soccer game. Or maybe your teacher gave you a lot of homework. These events can cause the amygdala to go into action.

Then what happens?

1. The amygdala sends a signal to the hypothalamus.

2. The hypothalamus sends a message to the pituitary gland.

3. The pituitary gland signals the adrenal glands, which are above your kidneys.

4. The adrenal glands release **hormones** into your blood.

Hormones cause the changes you feel in your body, like a faster heartbeat and breathing.

hypothalamus

2

1

signals

amygdala

3

pituitary
gland

adrenal
gland

4

kidney

stress ball

The prefrontal cortex also goes into action. This part of your brain helps you make good decisions. It helps you calm down. Maybe you want to yell or kick. But your prefrontal cortex tells you not to.

Sometimes your amygdala's reaction is stronger and faster. Anger takes over. If this happens, try to release some of your anger. How? Do jumping jacks, squeeze a stress ball, or yell into a pillow.

### SAFE ANGER

Anger becomes unsafe if **violence** is involved. If you think you or someone else might become violent, go to a safe place. Let a trusted adult know if you are having trouble controlling your anger or are worried about someone else's anger.

# MANAGE YOUR ANGER

It is normal to feel angry sometimes. It helps us know when something is unfair or unsafe. Notice how your body feels when you're angry. This will help you respond to anger in a healthy way. Sometimes, you may need to step away.

After you calm down, speak up. If you are mad at someone, let them know. Talking about your anger can help you feel better.

Getting angry too often can be bad for you. Learning how to **manage** it can keep both your mind and body healthy.

When you start to feel upset, take deep breaths. Count to 10. Say the ABCs to yourself. Repeat calming phrases like, "I will be OK."

Maybe you still think about something that made you upset a long time ago. Or maybe the same thing makes you angry again and again. Learn to let go of anger.

Ignoring anger isn't healthy. Talk to a trusted adult about your feelings. They can help you find a way to feel better.

**WRITE IT DOWN**

Writing about your feelings can help, too. Start a journal. Write in it when you feel angry. See if you notice any patterns.

Being **mindful** can also help you control your emotions. Slow down. Go outside. Enjoy what is around you. Studies show this can help develop the prefrontal cortex. It may help you have a healthier response to anger.

Everyone gets angry sometimes. Knowing what causes this feeling can help you stay calm. It can help you make good decisions.

# GOALS AND TOOLS

## GROW WITH GOALS

Understanding the changes that take place in your brain can help you take charge of your emotions and help you feel better when you're angry.

**Goal:** Understand what causes your anger.
Figure out what triggers you so you can be prepared.

**Goal:** Be mindful. Slow down and pay attention to what is around you. Practicing mindfulness can help train your brain to make good decisions.

**Goal:** Reflect on a time you got angry.
Do you think you handled the situation well?
What do you think you could have done differently?
What did you learn from the experience?

## TRY THIS!

Use positive self-talk. When you are upset, you may think things like, "I'm so angry. I hate this!" The next time you get angry, try thinking positively instead. Tell yourself things like, "I can handle this. I've got this. I will be OK. This will pass." Keep a list of positive sayings. Reread it when you need to remind yourself how to think when you get angry. Positive self-talk can help you better handle upsetting situations.

# GLOSSARY

**clench**
To close or hold tightly.

**emotion**
A feeling, such as happiness, sadness, or anger.

**energy**
The ability or strength to do things without getting tired.

**focuses**
Concentrates on something.

**frustrated**
Annoyed or angry.

**hormones**
Chemical substances made by your body that affect the way your body grows, develops, and functions.

**manage**
To succeed in something that is difficult.

**mindful**
A mentality achieved by focusing on the present moment and calmly recognizing and accepting your feelings, thoughts, and sensations.

**tense**
Stretched stiff and tight, or unable to relax.

**triggers**
Causes an action or emotion.

**unappreciated**
Not given recognition or thanks.

**violence**
The use of physical force to cause harm.

# TO LEARN MORE

## Finding more information is as easy as 1, 2, 3.

1. Go to www.factsurfer.com

2. Enter "**yourbrainwhenyou'reangry**" into the search box.

3. Choose your book to see a list of websites.

# INDEX

**adrenal glands** 10, 11

**amygdala** 8, 9, 10, 11, 13

**blood** 10

**body** 5, 7, 10, 14, 16

**brain** 7, 8, 13

**breathe** 7, 10, 16

**calm** 13, 15, 16, 20

**emotion** 4, 8, 20

**energy** 7

**face** 5

**fight, flight, or freeze response** 7

**frustrated** 4

**heart** 7, 10

**hormones** 10

**hypothalamus** 10, 11

**mindful** 20

**pituitary gland** 10, 11

**prefrontal cortex** 8, 13, 20

**talking** 15, 19

**tense** 5

**unappreciated** 4

**violence** 13

**vision** 7

**writing** 19

Blue Owl Books are published by Jump!, 5357 Penn Avenue South, Minneapolis, MN 55419, www.jumplibrary.com

Copyright © 2023 Jump! International copyright reserved in all countries. No part of this book may be reproduced in any form without written permission from the publisher.

Library of Congress Cataloging-in-Publication Data
Names: Colich, Abby, author.
Title: Your brain when you're angry / by Abby Colich.
Description: Minneapolis, MN: Jump!, Inc., [2023]
Series: Brainpower | Includes index.
Audience: Ages 7–10
Identifiers: LCCN 2022023394 (print)
LCCN 2022023395 (ebook)
ISBN 9798885241403 (hardcover)
ISBN 9798885241410 (paperback)
ISBN 9798885241427 (ebook)
Subjects: LCSH: Anger in children–Juvenile literature. | Anger–Physiological aspects–Juvenile literature. | Brain–Juvenile literature.
Classification: LCC BF723.A4 C645 2023 (print)
LCC BF723.A4 (ebook)
DDC 155.4/1247–dc23/eng/20220615
LC record available at https://lccn.loc.gov/2022023394
LC ebook record available at https://lccn.loc.gov/2022023395

Editor: Eliza Leahy
Designer: Emma Bersie

Photo Credits: Veja/Shutterstock, cover; Krakenimages.com/Shutterstock, 1; Bangkok Click Studio/Shutterstock, 3; Odua Images/Shutterstock, 4; AaronAmat/iStock, 5 (girl); sevenke/Shutterstock, 5 (background); Gatot Adri/Shutterstock, 6–7; DiversityStudio/Shutterstock, 8; ADDICTIVE STOCK CREATIVES/Alamy, 9; Shutterstock, 10–11; Mshev/Shutterstock, 12–13; nakaridore/Shutterstock, 14; eddiesimages/iStock, 15 (kids); CEW/Shutterstock, 15 (background); Pollyana Ventura/iStock, 16–17; grandriver/iStock, 18–19; AnnaStills/Shutterstock, 20–21.

Printed in the United States of America at Corporate Graphics in North Mankato, Minnesota.